SISTER GIRL
and the New Dress

By Nicole Fenner

Illustrated by Abira Das

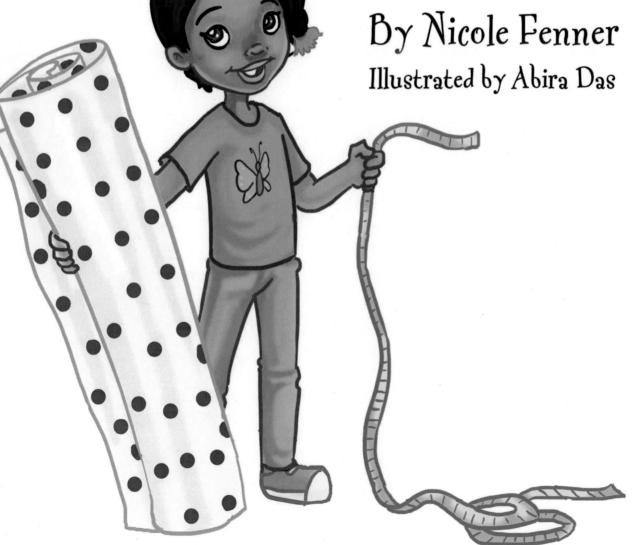

Printed in the United States of America

ISBN : 978-0578-454993

Library of Congress Control Number : 2016920011
Sister Girl Publishing PO Box 811, Halifax, NC 27839

Sistergirlpublishing@gmail.com

Sister Girl and the New Dress
is dedicated to our mothers, grandmothers,
sisters, aunts, cousins, caregivers and friends that
pour their hearts into being seamstress for their families.

We appreciate your love, creative expression, and support.
Thank you, mommy, you are appreciated.

Sitting at the kitchen table mixing chocolate chip cookie dough with Mom, Sister Girl daydreamed about the awards day on the last day of school. Sister Girl was so excited that she asked mom for a new pretty purple dress.

Sister Girl had the sweetest mother ever. Her mom was a very talented lady who loved children and loved helping the elderly. Sister Girl knew that when the season changed mother always sewed cute new outfits for her to wear.

In the winter, her mom sewed corduroy pants in a rainbow of colors.

In the summer, her mom prepared cute girly shorts and tank top sets with the brightest of pink, purple, and red hues for Sister Girl. It was amazing to Sister Girl how beautiful the clothes were.

Sister Girl's mom was a fashion queen with the sewing machine. Anything you wanted, her mom could make.

Sister Girl asked her mother, "How do you create such beautiful clothes?" Mom replied, "With an eye for fashion, patience to create, and taste to pull together the colors of the color wheel, I design beautiful clothes" Sister Girl looked at her mom in awe. "Where did you learn to be so creative?"

"Sister Girl, it's a combination of taking classes and trying new things on my own, and seeing what I like," she said.

Sister Girl asked her mother, "Can you teach me how to sew?"

Sister Girl said, in her very inquisitive and excitable voice, "Teach me! Teach me, Mommy! I am ready to learn!"

Mom told Sister Girl to pack her book bag and bring her snacks because they were taking a trip to the city to pick out a dress.

Sister Girl thought to herself, "Why would we need to pick out a dress if my mom is teaching me how to sew?"

She put her book bag on her back and walked with Mother to the train. They got off at the Fifth Avenue train Station between Broadway and Madison. It was a great Saturday evening. The City was bustling with ladies in the latest fashions in all shapes and sizes.

Sister Girl thought to herself, "It is a great day to find a new dress."
Sister Girl continued to walk down the street hand in hand with
her mom, smiling and humming the latest tunes she heard on the
radio the day before.

Finally they arrived at their destination.
It was a fabric store.
Sister Girl became very excited and ran into the store.

To Sister Girl's amazement there were bundles and bundles of fabric. There were warm hues of shiny silks fit for a queen, sequins that sparkled from across the room, plus cottons that felt so soft they slipped right through Sister Girl's fingers.

There were polyesters, rayons, satins, corduroys—every type of fabric you can imagine.

From behind the counter came the owner named Aaron who knew Mom very well. He said, "Liz, how can I help you today?"

Mom proceeded to tell Aaron that she is teaching Sister Girl how to sew, and that they are going to make a dress.

Aaron was so happy to assist Sister Girl. He asked , "What is your favorite color?" Sister Girl replied, "Purple."

"Purple is a royal color, Sister Girl," said Aaron. "That is very nice. I will pull out all the purple fabrics, and you can choose what you like."

After walking around the store, Mom decided that she needed two yards of the purple velvet fabric for the dress, and one yard of white silk with purple polka dots, as well.

Sister Girl could not contain her excitement. She jumped up and down, oohing and aahing at the counter, while Aaron cut the fabric.

Aaron asked, "Do you lovely ladies need any additional supplies today for your project?"

Mom replied, "Yes, we will need some purple thread, needles, measuring tape, and a cup of smiles."

The fabric store owner laughed and said, "Coming right up!"

Sister Girl asked her mom, "Why do we need the additional supplies?"

Mom replied, "To make your dress, we need the thread to hold the fabric together, the needles to hold the thread and sew the dress, and the measuring tape so I can measure you and draw the pattern to design your dress."

They walked down the street to the local bakery and ordered a couple of delectable rainbow cookies, and two cheese Danishes.

While sitting at the table eating their sweets, Sister Girl told Mom how excited she was to learn how to sew.

Mother told Sister Girl she must be patient, and they finished up their afternoon snacks and headed back home on the train.

When they arrived home, Mom and Sister Girl laid the fabric on the sewing table , and Mom rolled the sewing machine out to start on the project with Sister Girl. Sister Girl was anxious and excited all at the same time.

Mom said, "Stand up, Sister Girl, I need to take your measurements."
So Sister Girl stood up, and Mom took her measurements.
Sister Girl asked, "Why do you need to measure me?"

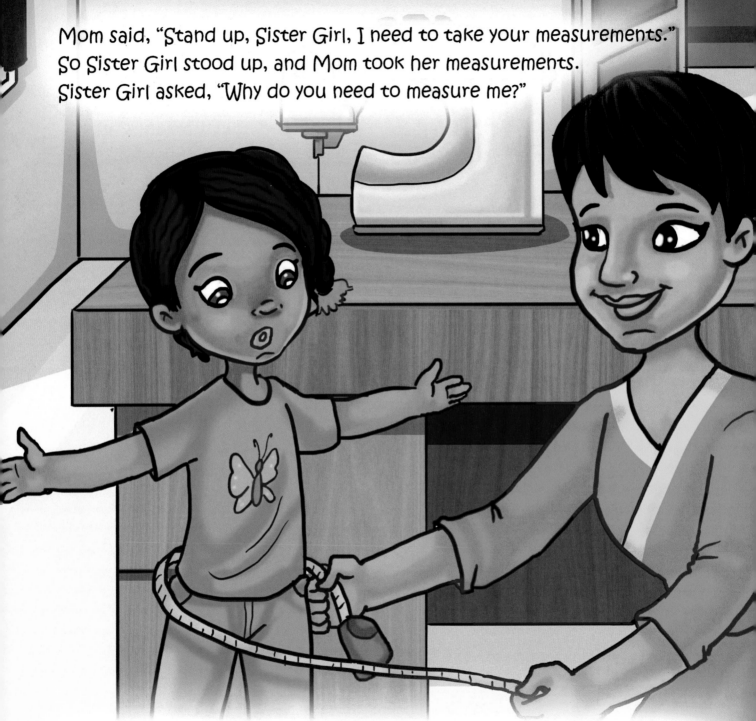

Mom replied, "So I can see how long to cut your sleeves, find the width of the dress, and create the minor details." Sister Girl just smiled in amazement.

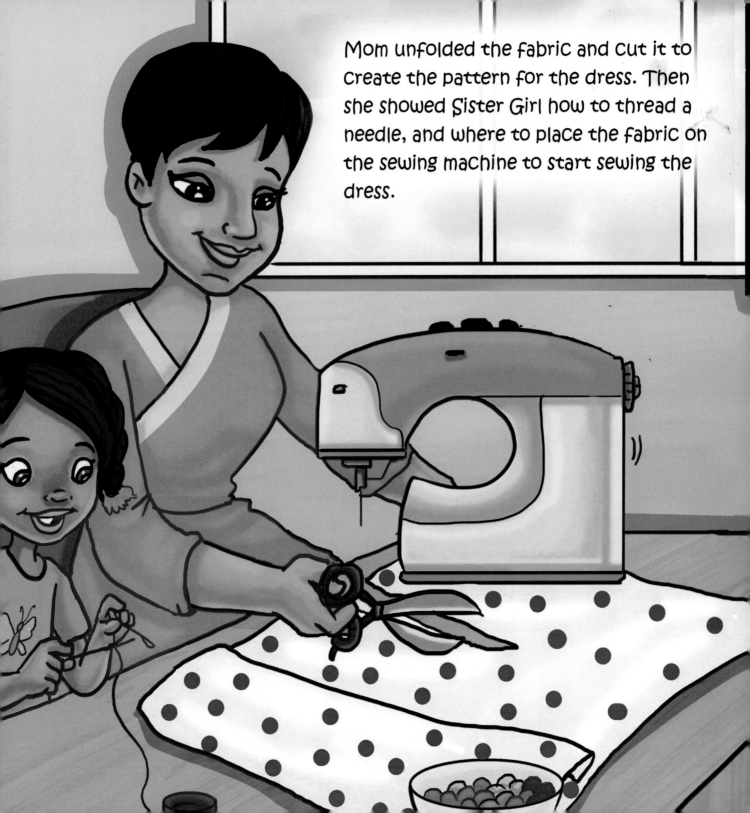

Mom unfolded the fabric and cut it to create the pattern for the dress. Then she showed Sister Girl how to thread a needle, and where to place the fabric on the sewing machine to start sewing the dress.

After a couple of hours the dress was complete.

It was the prettiest dress Sister Girl had ever laid her eyes on. It had a white silk top with purple polka dots, a cute purple rose on the right side of the chest, and a silky, shiny belt around the waist that tied into a wonderful bow in the back. The knee length skirt of the dress was made from the finest purple velvet.

Sister Girl was so happy that she had learned a new skill, plus her beautiful dress was ready for the awards day on the last day of school.

Mom told Sister Girl, "We are not quite done yet. Please get the scissors and the ironing board, because we must cut the loose threads and iron the dress to perfection."

After completing the final phase of sewing, Sister Girl tried on her new dress. She exuded so much pride and grace. Sister Girl smiled from ear to ear. Mom said, "What a beauty!"

Monday morning Sister Girl woke up very excited. She was going to wear her new dress to school. Sister Girl went to the mirror, brushed her ponytail, put on her lip gloss, slid on her cat eye glasses, shined her shoes, and put on her lace ruffled socks.

She was ready for school. Before running out the door to catch the bus, Sister Girl grabbed her mom and smiled. "Thank you," Sister Girl said to Mom.

When Sister Girl arrived at school all the little girls complimented her dress and asked where she had bought it.
Sister Girl batted her eyes, smiled, and said, "My mother taught me how to sew. I made the dress myself. Come over after school and I will teach you too."

Made in the USA
Middletown, DE
22 September 2021